Watercolor Eyes

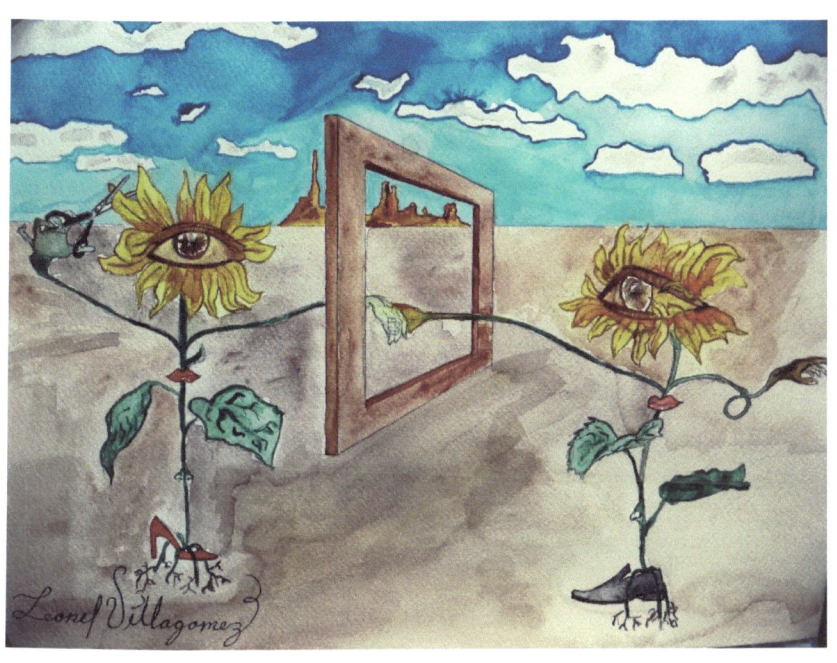

Leonel & Joshi Villagomez

Watercolor Eyes by Leonel Villagomez & Joshi Villagomez
Independently Published. Seattle WA, USA.

www.joshivillagomez.com
&
www.villagomezart.com

Copyright © 2019 Leonel Villagomez & Joshi Villagomez

All rights reserved. No portion of this book may be reproduced in any form without permission from the publisher or the author, except as permitted by U.S. copyright law. For permissions, contact:

writervillagomez@gmail.com

Art and Cover by Leonel Villagomez

ISBN: 9781796613308

2nd Revision. First published on: February 12, 2019

WATERCOLOR EYES

By

Leonel & Joshi Villagomez

Leonel & Joshi Villagomez

Watercolor Eyes

Recipe to hallucinate

50 ounces of time
20 ounces of rejoicing
A 12-inch ruler
A squad
1 caliper
1 flower (fragrance and color as desired)
1 liter of joy
1 glass of water
½ spoonful of sea salt
3 kilos of freedom
The melody of Saint-Saëns's *Samson and Delilah*, Op. 47
A photograph (preferably one that inspires you)
A spoon of energy (especially from the sun)
7 memories (recommend: those that make you laugh to get oxygen)
6 elements of love (to maximize flavor)
9 ants
2 dragonflies
And 28 lice

Leonel & Joshi Villagomez

D'Art Content

- I. Life
- II. The Beginning
- III. Sweet Window
- IV. Friendship Between the Giraffe and the Rose
- V. The Muse
- VI. The Golden Hair Harp
- VII. Mr. Roberto
- VIII. With Elevation to Heaven
- IX. Ivory Musical Strings
- X. The Art Curator
- XI. The Ear of Van Gogh
- XII. Virgin Sofia
- XIII. Conquest
- XIV. A Colorful Dream
- XV. The Beauty of Music
- XVI. The Echo of Heaven
- XVII. Confusion of Time
- XVIII. The Extravagance of Saí
- XIX. The Artistic Mirage
- XX. Letter to Juliet
- XXI. Other Works of Art
- XXII. Replicas
- XXIII. Biographies

I.
Life

Life is happiness because we live surrounded by art. Magical seasons, pleasurable climates, magnificent sunrises, and unforgettable evenings. We inhabit an impressive place that shelters surreal creatures such as the giraffe, elephant, kangaroo, rhinoceros, eagle, peacock, narwhal, and more.

We are surrounded by incredible mountains, colorful singing birds, old trees, rivers, lakes, beautiful waterfalls, and everything that our eyes can appreciate. Our eyes are delighted daily with the beauty that surrounds us. But within all this beauty, there is a difference in how we appreciate art.

Art has existed for millennia and has been a unique and unmistakable means of expression. Despite the extravagance in the style of some artists, you can meticulously observe a message spread between those brushstrokes and those molded sculptures.

Unlike other forms of expression, art is created without rules and ordinances. It needs no introductions or abbreviations: art is only exhibited. Illustrations, color, or form let the mind discern the objective of the artist through his work.

Unlike a hundred-year-old oak tree or a rocky mountain, the artistic work is appreciated in a different way. Watercolor eyes will follow lines, shape, texture, color, and style. Those eyes are diffused within the level of art to appreciate the delicacy of the work.

Appreciating art is not easy, as it involves a series of discernments and understandings. To distinguish one artist from another, it is necessary to broaden one's knowledge in art and see through those magnificent eyes the definition and message in artwork.

LIFE is happiness, but you have to learn to appreciate it with the retina of your eyes. Amplify your appreciation of the order of life, through those horizon lines that mark a division between land and sky. Look around for a second. And look at how the lines are drawn through those square walls, those vertical chairs and tables, the plasma television, the separation of the concrete floor from the earth, the uniform division that the tree makes by obstructing the vision, the line on the horizon that is made from the division of the mountains and the clouds behind them, the line on the horizon that is made on the beach with the sea and the sky above it, and the symmetrical division of your mother's face, of your father's, of yourself.

In the same way that our bodies get used to the timbre of voice, language, culture, and food, in the same way the eyes appreciate a raft in the immensity of the ocean. We are gratified to see it. By appreciating life, we understand that life is beautiful.

Watercolor Eyes

II.
The Beginning

The beginning of all art starts with what you want to express. This is true whether you are a designer, sculptor, architect, barista, painter, or anything that involves a little artistic development.

Based on this desire, the artist, or the author of the expressive message, looks for the medium in which he will express a little of what he has in mind.

The fashion designer looks for the texture of the fabric that combines the extravagance of the design and the season of the year in which this work is expected to be shared.

The sculptor seeks to combine the aesthetic value of the work, with the weight, duration, and climatic exposure in which this work will be exhibited.

The architect brings lines together with calculations that give life to the building that creates a welcoming and perhaps extravagant refuge.

A barista expands his feelings, emotions, and time to draw a heart or other image over the coffee.

And the painter carries his expression and imagination over those linear, irregular, geometric, or uniform strokes. He gives life, color, something realistic, or something imaginary.

Watercolor Eyes

In any case, the expression is carried out with the desire to articulate knowledge and ideas. The practice of art applies to most jobs, as long as you consider it an art.

In the following painting entitled **"The Beginning,"** you can see horizontal and vertical lines. The religious and divine touch in the upper part of the art is exposed between two architectural columns of Roman style; below that, its influence is visualized with a trumpet and an angel above the forehead of the human being.

In this painting, the Villagomez's connection with the Roman, religious, and spiritual impressions is discovered. And in turn, the message can be interpreted as a connection of God through sound. Of course, that is the ambiguous interpretation I give you. For any work of art is open to self-interpretation through those watercolor eyes.

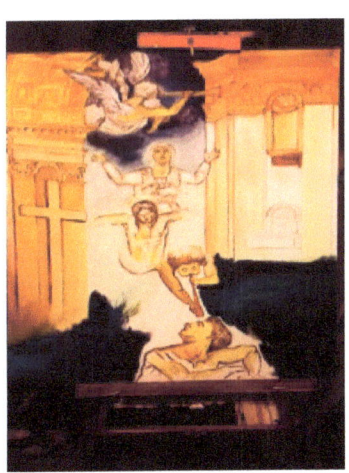

III.
Sweet Window

In order to appreciate art, we must first know the methods used. How much did the artist work to carry the idea, and how much time could have been taken to achieve it? Having a little knowledge of the methods used, or having a close notion, helps the viewer appreciate the work of art in a meaningful way.

The value of the next painting will increase, as it has become part of the artist's signature style. Despite having no precise value at the moment, this painting could become worth thousands, if not millions, as it becomes part of the artist's aesthetic stamp in other of his works (later, I will explain in detail).

Art, as mentioned above, is the total expression of form and thought. The piece of art below has a surrealist distinction, yet also a sense of truth, when the observer knows the origins of the work.

The fruit of the Pyrus, or pear tree, is the central fragment of this work of art. Let's observe how the realist division, with a little effort, becomes part of a surrealist message. It tunes in not only to the feelings of the artist of the work, but also those of the observer. What do you see?

Watercolor Eyes

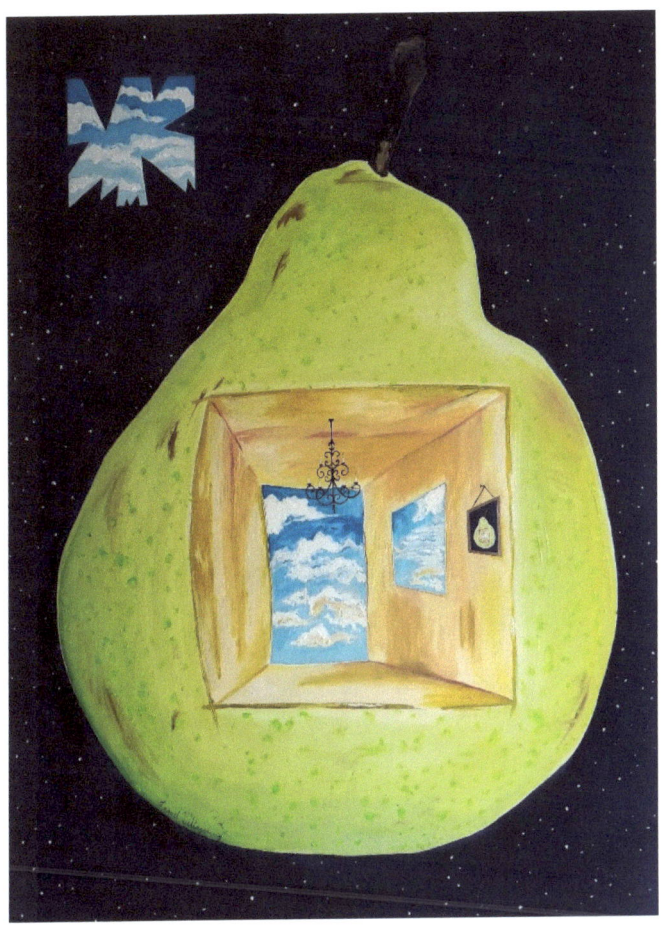

The work, as you can see, has a true effect within the imagination. Its contrast of colors relative to nature captivates the mind. Within its simplicity, there is an elixir that penetrates the natural sensations of the spectator, since it opens his mind to the relative and the different.

Leonel & Joshi Villagomez

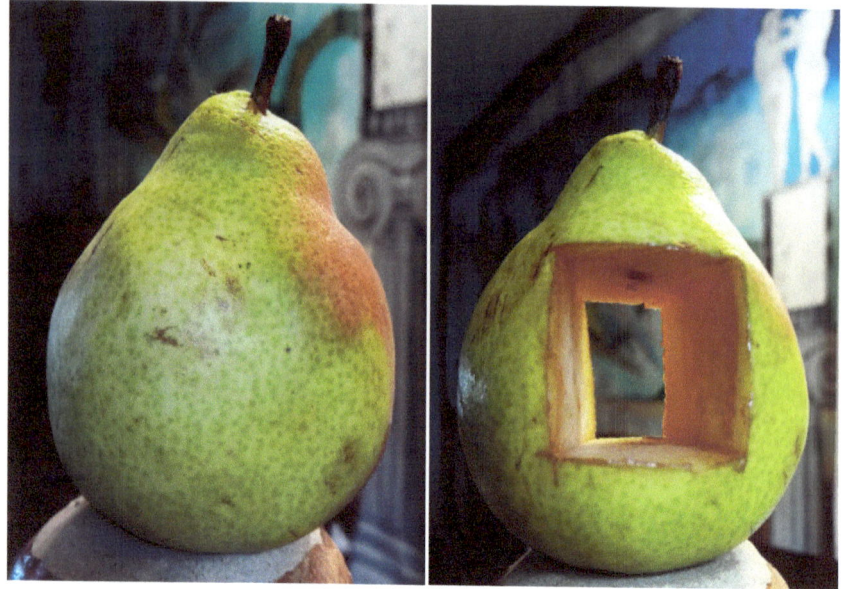

IV.
Friendship Between the Giraffe and the Rose

Beyond the realistic description of creations, there is surrealism within life. The theme, divided into realism and imagination, opens doors to a strange and parallel world where reality itself does not need collective exaltation, for its own nature makes your eyes shine enigmatically. And it inclines our eyes to what seems to be magnified. Look, for example, at the neck of the giraffe in the painting below.

Villagomez takes again an extravagant creation of life and expands it by opening doors and windows over the giraffe. As you can see on the next page and by comparing with the previous painting, the surrealist work on **"Friendship Between the Giraffe and the Rose"** has a representation over the earth and not outside the atmosphere as **"Sweet Window."**

Does the giraffe intend to eat the rose? Of course not. That is not the intention. In this painting, you can see that the giraffe has come a long way just to talk to her friend the rose. Something unimaginably subliminal: true friendship is presented in a surreal, detailed, and intimate way.

In the previous chapter, we learned the process of **"The Sweet Window."** For the current painting, it would be curious, pleasant, but ultimately unimaginable to think that the author could have used a giraffe to paint this work. Could it be? Does the artist have a giraffe as a pet? Questions like these broaden the interest and value of art. They build knowledge as an art connoisseur.

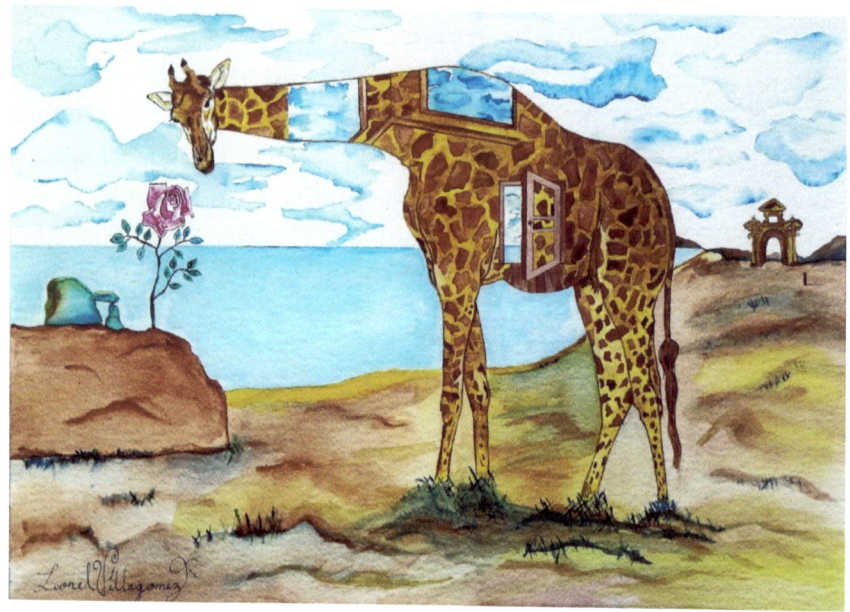

V.
The Muse

In this oil painting, we can see the excessive combination of certain physical traits that differentiate people. Again, exaggeration of beauty is not done with a realistic or photographic style, but with a surreal and imaginary style. It reflects the idea that a woman's hair tends to be an essential part of her person. Without focusing in other details, this painting exaggerates this trait, because after all, each personality is identified with personal style.

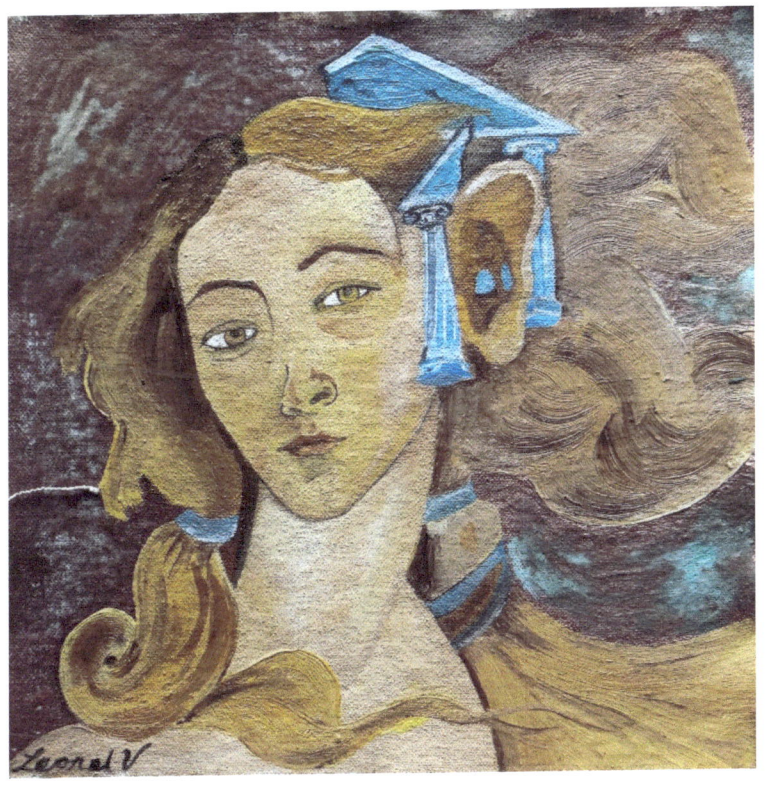

Observe the combination of your own hair with your eyes, and how those extend your traits to a distinctive level of art.

Throughout history, we have witnessed the value women have on beauty. Art and beauty. Women and art. A touch in which colors, attitudes, identifying traits, and personality are exchanged. The imposing beauty in art is in its colors, its message, the mechanisms of its creation, and its destiny.

VI.
The Golden Hair Harp

Here again we see an appreciation of art, beauty, and personal traits that are valuable for personal recognition. Again, we see a connection between the real and the surreal. Why?

While to the eyes of many this symbolizes a musical instrument, and whose title is precisely that, to many others this work of art may be the gentleness with which one caresses the hair of someone beloved. Here we see how the elements of attraction take possession through action—through the love and care given to that special person.

And this is how the watercolor eyes are put into practice, to look in detail at the outline of things and look at them differently. Reality is the same. And the appreciation of surrealism depends on you.

Leonel & Joshi Villagomez

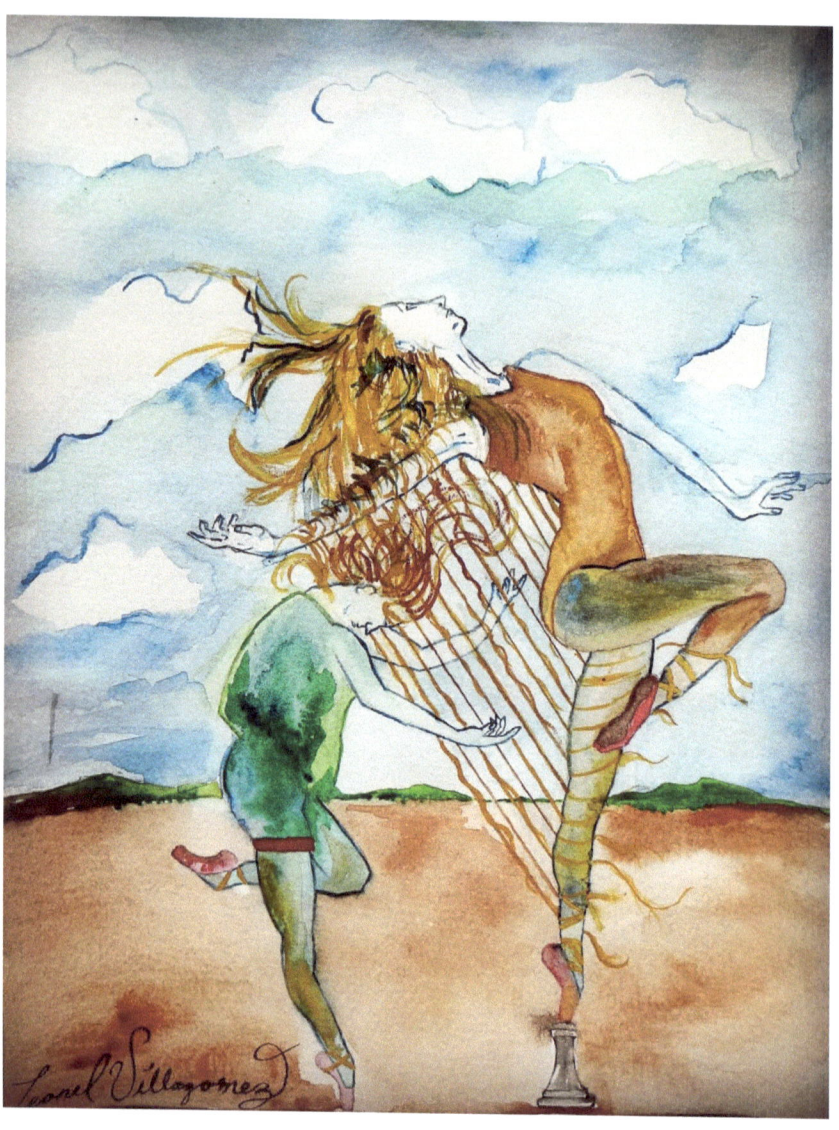

VII.
Mr. Roberto

The divinity of things, the appreciation of art, the interest of life, the distinction of the necessary with the secondary, the personality mentality, and the purpose of life are influenced by the wise: by those who have lived longer and learned through the years.

While rational knowledge hardly lasts more than eighty years, the teachings of fathers, grandparents, and ancestors endure through new generations.

In this portrait, observe how the gentle attitude of long years past stares into the present. The slight inclination of his back shows the tiredness of his years; nevertheless, the artist maintains a lifelike brightness in the man's eyes.

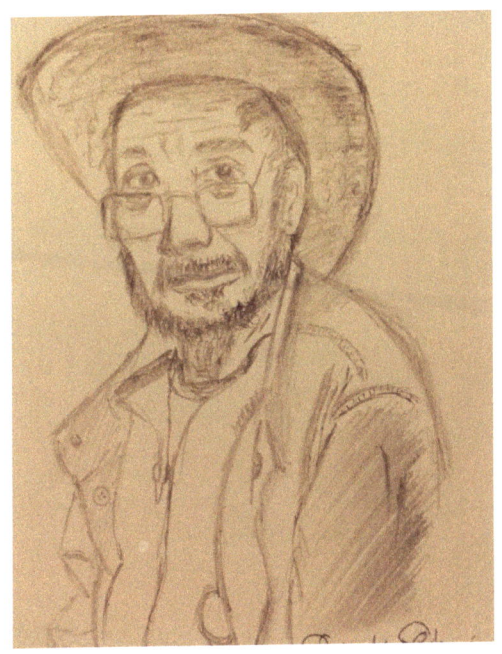

And this is how certain details, not presented photographically, amplify the message of the work.

VIII.
With Elevation to Heaven

Some artistic projects take more imagination than others. Compared to a portrait, or the specific explosion of methodical elements, the imagination of Villagomez is presented in his works. The value of imagination in art corresponds to its originality, appreciation of detail, symbolism, message, and what it represents in time. Outside of the consideration that art is valuable because it is generated individually or *en masse*, the imagination it takes to make the piece raises the value of the work.

In the following images observe how the complexity of the work relies on steps generated from the planning of the idea to the concretization of the piece. The artist uses mathematical modifications and imaginary concepts.

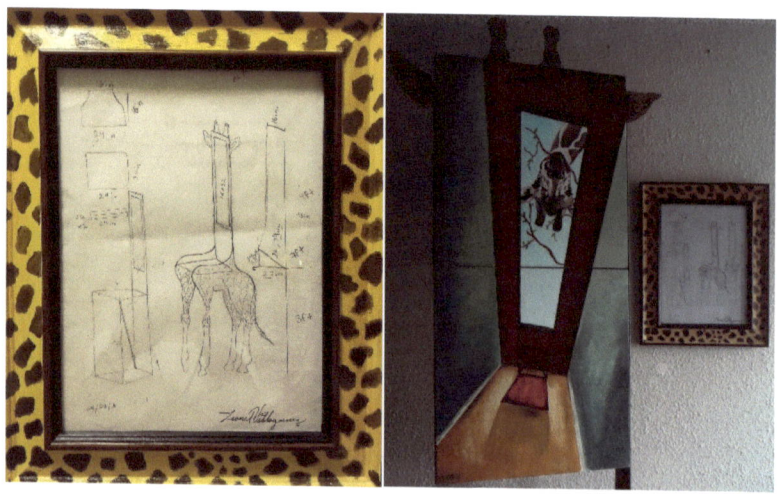

Watercolor Eyes

The value of art and its appreciation are measured by the combination of existing elements and the creativity in how the work is put to use. This means that a chair, normally a mundane object, can become a symbol of artistic attention.

Imagination is necessary to observe and appreciate the work of an artist. And in this case, I am not referring to the imagination used to create the work of art, but to one's own imagination that elevates itself toward an idea of how the work of art was created. The observer appreciates the complete work using his eyes, those watercolor eyes.

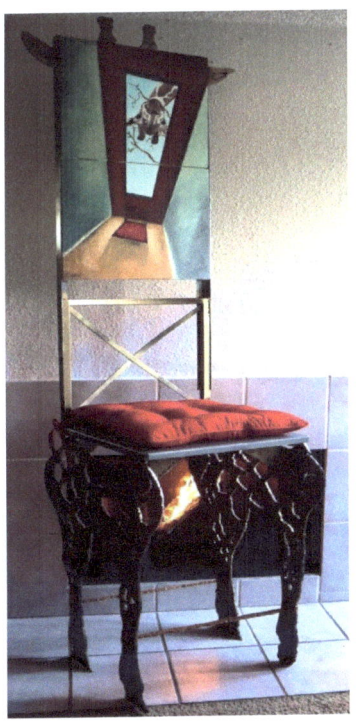

IX.
Ivory Musical Strings

The style the artist Villagomez is generated through various created pieces. The diatonic formation, in music as in art, is a long and persevering process. The artist's discipline and constant integration of his experience with his imagination can be observed as drops of appropriation in his artistic works.

An artist is not made from one day to the next. It requires consistent practice to generate the style and imagination needed to create a unique work.

Similarly, for every art connoisseur, knowledge and appreciation of art is born from that pedagogical interest in artistic creation. The focus on elements and methodology depend on recognizing the majestic value of art. Without these, it is difficult to understand or imagine the steps the artist could have taken.

Watercolor Eyes

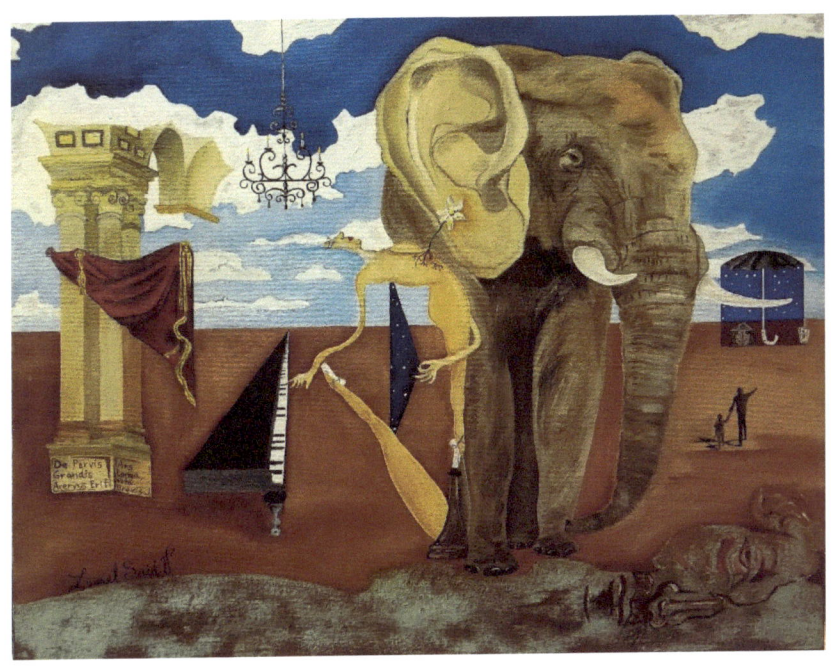

"I want to get high on consciousness to see every color and detail. To breathe deeply, to be a genius of memory, to listen to every drop of water in the middle of the rain, to feel the freshness of the wind, and to feel the beating of the trees. I am tired of living in my sleep.

"My conscience I give to you because it was yours and will always be yours. When I get angry, I miss the opportunity to learn, so I will always be happy, but it also has to be crazy, because I want to be crazy excited and travel to the corners of the earth and explore, but more than that to another dimension without having to move time.

Leonel & Joshi Villagomez

"I can have wings like angels. The secret is imagination. I'll never stop laughing, but laughing sadly, that college never taught me that to be exciting is like the 'magic' of being a genius. I am almost certain that Beethoven conferred with the heavens and the earth to create the 9th Symphony because at the hour of his agony he was applauded.

"And at the hour of my agony I want the angels to take me by the arms and the giraffes to speak to me and the elephants to fly and the ants to accompany me and St. Peter to open the gates without having to look for my name." –Leonel

X.
The Art Curator

In the same way as the previous painting, we may begin to recognize the artist's style, for the next painting maintains the same style. Unlike the other works that bear his signature, this work of art has a specific trait of Villagomez. What is it?

I invite you to observe the painting for a minute and tell me what it is. We observe the molding of the elements that have created the artist's distinctive and peculiar style. The central part of this painting is a sculpture titled **"The Echo of Heaven,"** which appears later in this book. In the sculpture, images of writers such as Edgar Allan Poe and Gabriel García Márquez appear emerging as from the thoughts of the figure's mind. They indicate how significant it is to learn, and by learning, to overcome the limits of one's own style and creativity.

But the specific feature to which I refer in this painting is the replication, in the right side, of the painting **"The Sweet Window"** (discussed earlier in this book). This tiny replication of a previous idea within a new idea is a significant symbol. It corresponds to the majestic, personal touch of Villagomez. Imagine that the artist creates 100 new ideas and in all of them similarly replicates **"The Sweet Window."** What would be the value of the original work?

The value of art, as I have explained before, depends on several factors. But the most important is the essence of the artist in his works.

Pablo Picasso's style differs from that of Vincent Van Gogh, and so on for the differences between every artist. That is why the artist's style and what the artist represents can be perceived in their numerous works of art (even though they are different). And in the same way, the value of art is integrated with that value of history.

Watercolor Eyes

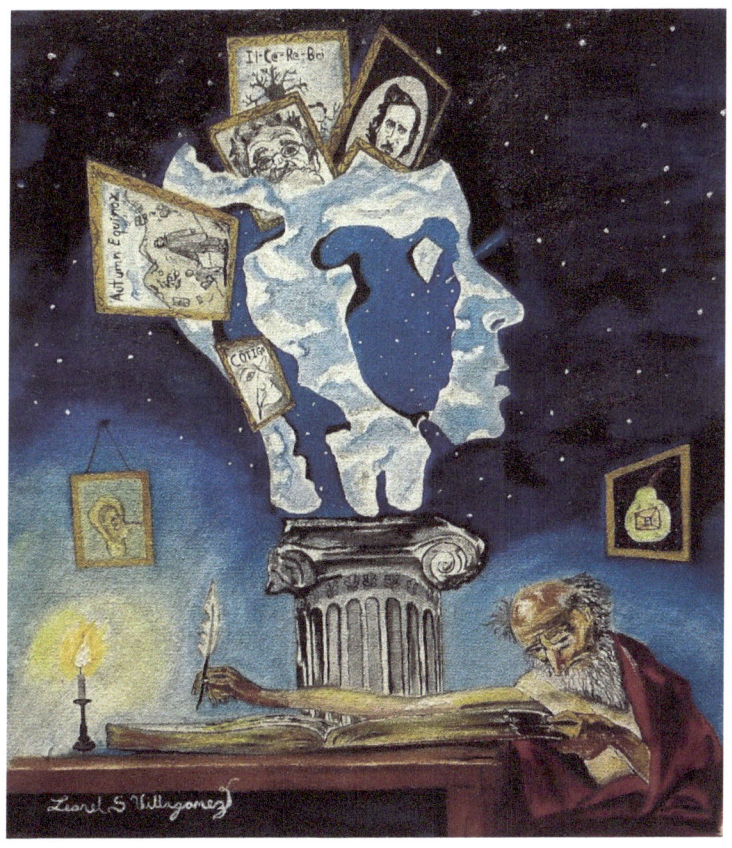

XI.
The Ear of Van Gogh

In order to learn to appreciate art, it is necessary to know about art. That is to say, we must learn its basic contexts: who was the author of the work, in which year it was created, where did it originate, and so on. This information is fundamental to recognize contemporary or centuries-old artists and their works.

Knowing the history of art broadens your appreciation of those works exhibited before you. And that's because if you know Vincent Van Gogh, your reaction to the next painting would be more intimate.

The following painting is a portrait of the Dutch painter, who was born in 1853. It imitates Van Gogh's special, identifiable style, while adding the personal touches of the artist Leonel Villagomez. The work emerges entirely from his inspiration from and connection to artists like Van Gogh.

The difference is clear, as Van Gogh's own style is not wholly reflected in this work of art—for instance, by not exposing the brushstrokes in the way that characterized the Dutch artist's prodigy. Even so, this portrait is elevated with a series of techniques and styles characteristic of the artist and observable in his paintings in this book. Like the work **"Ivory Musical Strings,"** in this piece one can see a person standing in the distance, giving the impression that the portrait is possibly a sculpture and not a painting.

Watercolor Eyes

When the game of reality and illusion make a connection with the personal, a painting goes from being informative to being subjective. The emotions involved in the appreciation of art are important: the emotional sigh heralds the personal recognition of art. And so, despite (or in addition to) any given description of what a work "means," the viewer of art can generate his own interpretation.

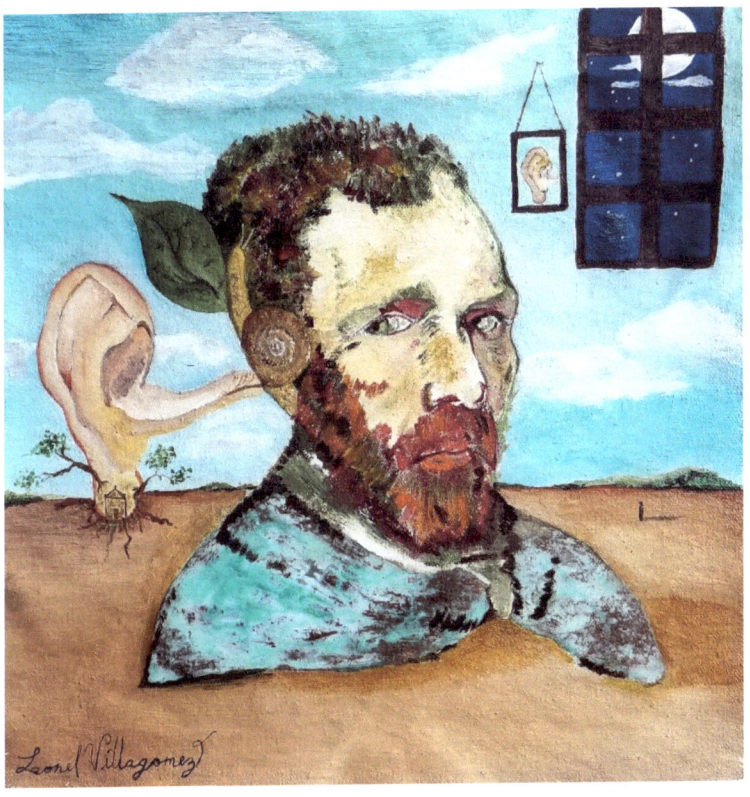

XII.
Virgin Sofia

Emotions maximize the fusion between the observer's eyes and the piece of art. Knowledge, experiences, and emotions open the discernment of art to another level. This helps us understand how each individual can appreciate art differently. While for one person a heart drawn on a leaf means love, for another person the same drawing can mean desolation.

The intricacy of feelings and emotions leads the observer of art to achieve a closer and more pleasant connection with the work of art. By drawing over his black and white eyes with a colorful landscape that exposes the meaning of the piece, the observer can appreciate the work of art on a personal level.

In the next piece, observe the sensuality of the brush-strokes mixed with the attractive colors. The cold of the river draws from the wind—water and breath, a combination of madness and reality. Like the words of this book, the image contains the natural and the fictitious dancing between what could be, what is, and what is coming.

The madness and sensuality of this piece is a clear example of how emotions can play an important role in savoring art. Fragile colors and the ideas of Villagomez are amplified by the viewer's knowledge and emotions, thus, giving the work the unmistakable value of subjectivity between the person and the work of art.

Watercolor Eyes

And this is how the combination of the elements the observer has learned about art begin to give life to those watercolor eyes. You don't need a master's degree in art, or many millions in your bank account, to learn to taste art. Knowledge is forged through the eye of the individual and their own way of appreciating art.

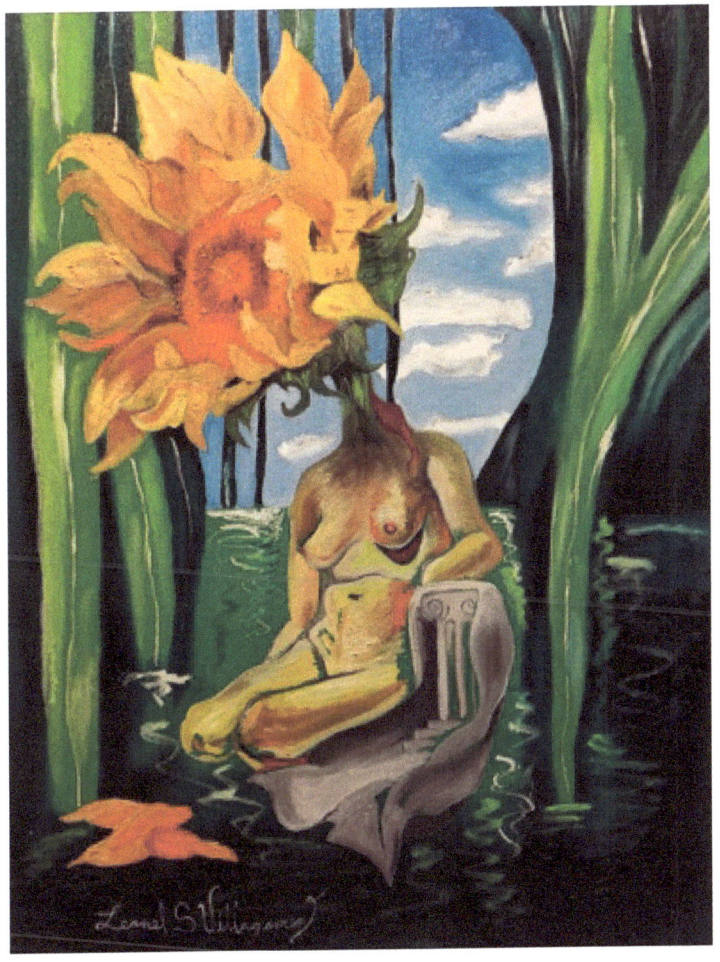

"Through all my artistic expression, and along with the literature of many writers who have inspired me and who have been protagonists of their own creative genius, I have realized that my artistic talent could be described as 'artistic madness,' and you can see how my technique has changed.

"The theme of my painting is constantly evolving. Plato, who distinguished between clinical madness and creative madness, said: 'The sight of a beautiful body awakens the burning desire for divine beauty, and it is when inspired people are brought into a state of divine madness.' From this theory emerges the idea that the artist's 'madness' is a necessary mechanism for artistic creation. In the same way, it is inevitable for me to have two different worlds, the real and the imaginary.

"The real world gives me all the resources to be able to subsist, and the imaginary world every day opens new doors and gives me the opportunity to explore my imagination and satisfy my artistic appetite.

"Throughout the history of art, we can observe through architecture, sculpture, painting, and of course literature, how the artist needs to manifest himself through his genius. And we can find an infinity of incredible works to imagine.

"For example, my most recent work, 'Virgin Sofia,' is inspired by the Mexican writer Jaime Sabines's poem 'Tía Chofi.' When I first heard this beautiful poem I was moved, and the only thing that came to mind was an illuminated

flower-woman living her first days to the last hour of her death without breaking her virgin skin.

"My desire to create this work was unconscious because Jaime Sabines recited it and with his own words said: 'You were always the same easy thing, like the flowers of the field.' This impelled me to imagine a picture with an enormous sunflower, representing the beauty that he carried in his face, and the naked body, the virgin body." –Leonel

XIII.
Conquest

After applying the techniques of art appreciation mentioned throughout this book, an affiliation or rapport between art and oneself is born. Like other ordinary things in other fields, it requires determination, dedication, and affection; but most of all, art appreciation requires passion. It is a mutual conquest—an agreeable one. "But I am not an artist!" one may say. Nevertheless, art has existed around us since before our birth and will continue until after our departure.

Remember that art exists in the trees, in the roots, in the plants, in the animals, in the birds, in the wind, and in everything that we consider vital for our existence and happiness. We unconsciously separate ourselves from art, despite depending on it daily.

The mutual conquest between oneself and art goes beyond sentimentalism, rationalism, spiritualism, Darwinism, or any other explanation contrived within the self. We live within art. Just stop for a second and think about what you like, and what you have done in recent years to sweeten your reality.

Beyond all the details of how art surrounds us, it is enough to say that learning to appreciate art begins with paying close attention to oneself. When wearing red slippers, when wearing black shoes, or when deciphering a magnificent connection with someone who was once a stranger.

Watercolor Eyes

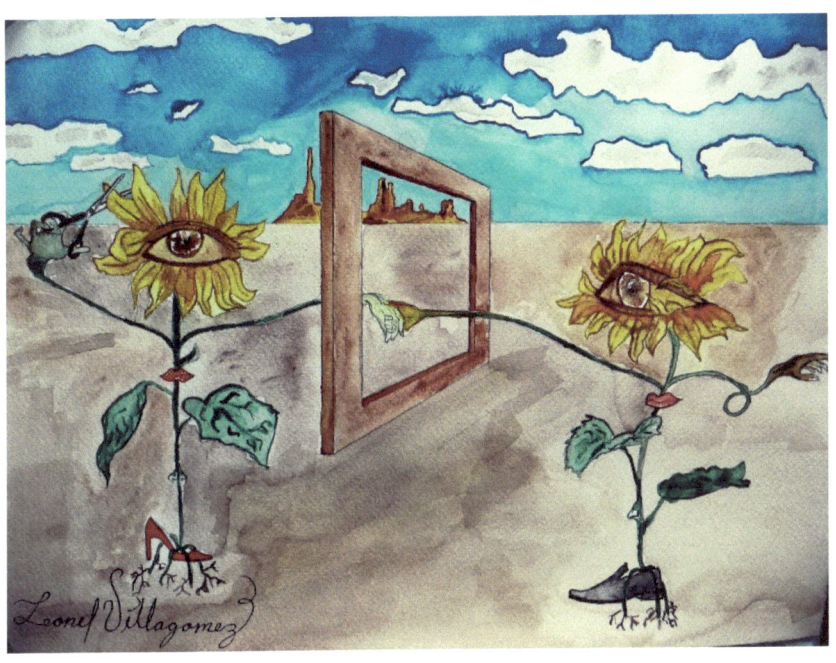

XIV.
A Colorful Dream

The reality and the lie are both lived with purpose. If you make yourself lie just to smile, then do it. Personal madness spreads as we appreciate that which surrounds us. And the lie should be taken up not to deceive, but to make someone happy.

Truth and lies in a work of art depend on the composition of realistic and imaginary elements. A green whale, for example, will look like a lie or a deception within the realm of what we merely know. However, it broadens the imagination of the observer to the point of making him think or smile. Specific features such as these emerge from the personal touch and style of the artist: their particular distortion of the truth.

Life is like that. And that is why life is art. Not everything is true, and not everything is a lie. One lives happily in one time and smiles through lies at another time. The appreciation of art depends on how it is observed, understood, and valued. The enigmatic tones that contain the artist's clear message can always be open to interpretation, giving it the exuberance necessary for it to become part of you.

Watercolor Eyes

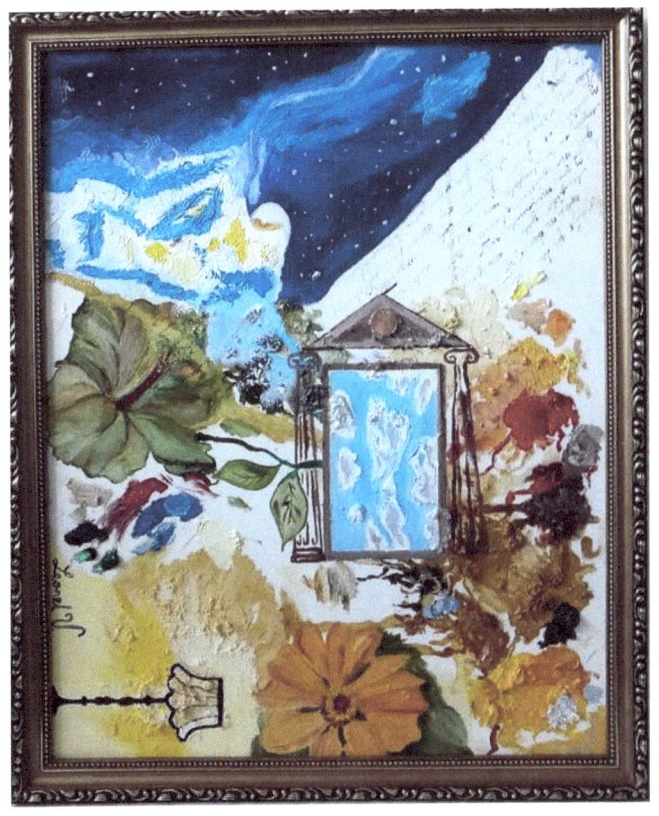

XV.
The Beauty of Music

There is music within the fine visual arts. It is not unusual for most visual artists to strive to transfer the magic of music to something tangible. In the following work, observe the artist's connection with music. Whether directly or indirectly, instruments play an important role in the style of Villagomez, and they can be observed throughout his works.

Unlike **"The Golden Hair Harp,"** this work represents a single individual. The diaphanous rhythm makes light an ordinary occasion and personalizes it. Again, within this piece we have an example of how a specific work of art can add personal and emotional meaning.

Those watercolor eyes are not born without the constant appreciation of art on an interpersonal, intellectual, and descriptive level. They grow by invoking, with subliminal tones, the deep desire to appreciate art.

Watercolor Eyes

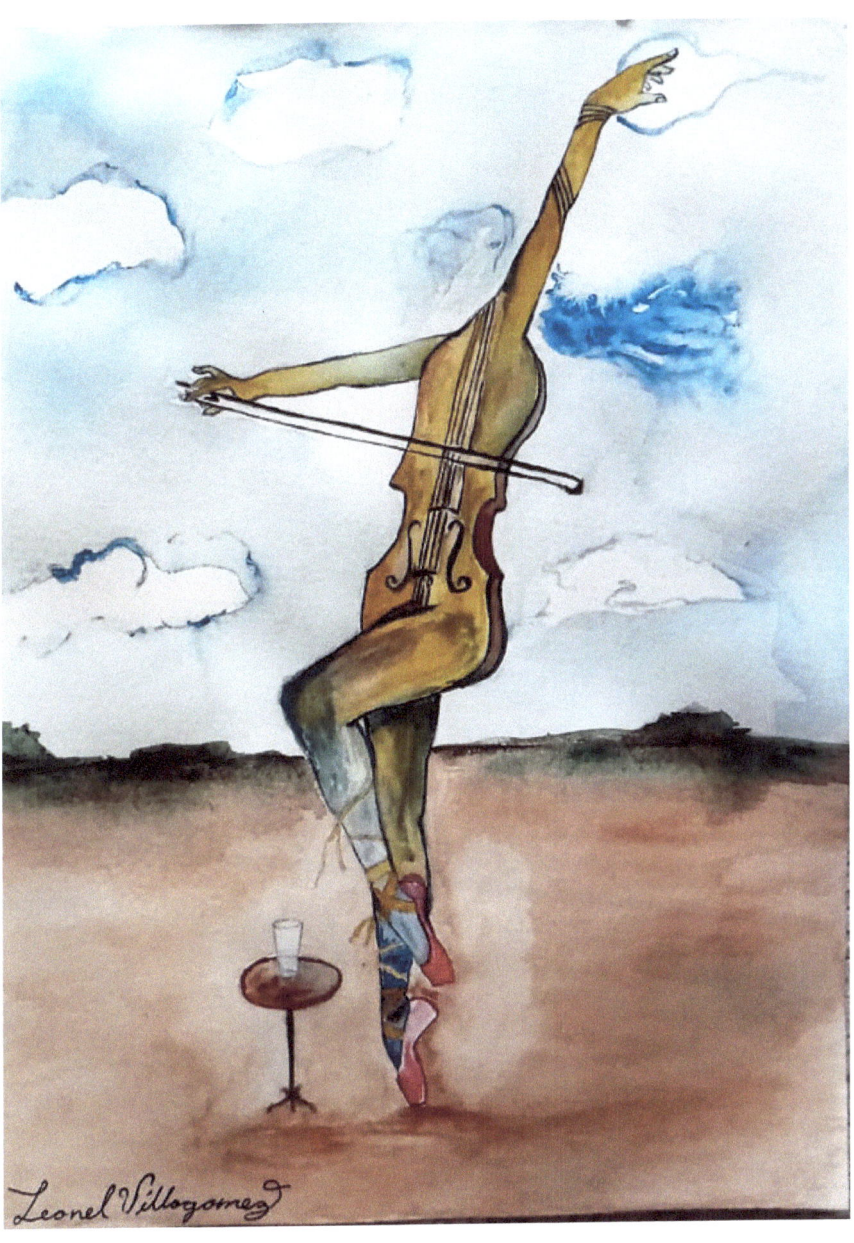

XVI.
The Echo of Heaven

Art, as I mentioned at the beginning, exists in various forms and styles. Besides painting, another expressive style of the visual artist is sculpture. The piece shown below has a symbolic and personal value present in other works by Villagomez. Earlier in this book, you will notice how this sculpture is a central part of another of his paintings. Perhaps it is not the central message, but even so, it becomes a transcendental value.

The following sculpted works show once again the surrealist style of Villagomez. The personification of himself in art can be perceived in the extravagantly molded sculptures and in the little starry universe within the piece.

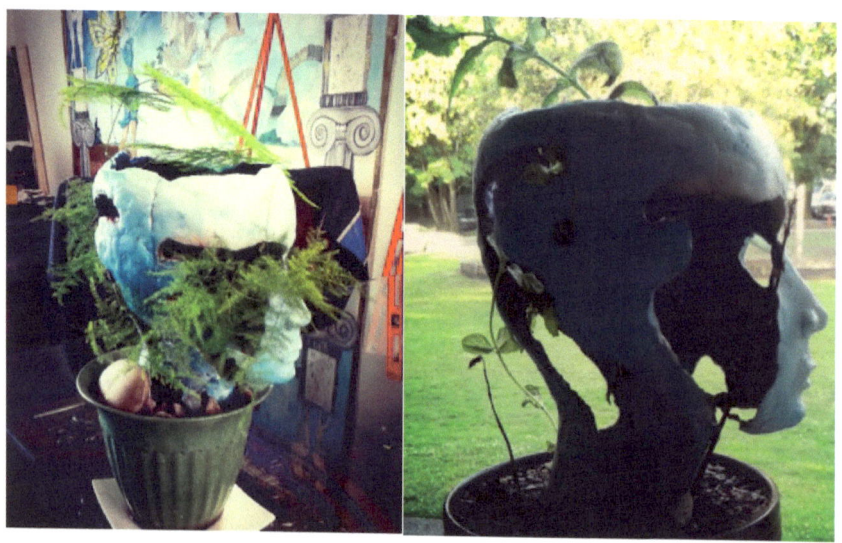

Watercolor Eyes

Details such as the universe painted inside the head add surrealistic reality: one can imagine the connection between the millions of stars in the night sky with the millions of neurons in the human mind. Again, this is a piece that exposes the artist's genuine imagination and provokes the viewer's own imagination.

XVII.
Confusion of Time

Unlike "The Echo of Heaven," the following sculptures ("Golden Roman Column," "Blending Cultures," and "The Mandate of Caesar") have not been painted. Even so, one can observe how historical events or buildings such as those present in Villagomez's paintings are taken up again with a surrealistic touch.

The separation of space and geometric form broadens the viewer's imagination to observe in detail the generic features of the Villagomez's style on a three-dimensional level.

We live within the minds of several artists. Like waking up every morning and seeing a roof over us, we live within their influence. Even by observing in detail the molded earth composites in our homes and paying attention to how we use them, we apprehend how a sculpture forged by the naked idea is a three-dimensional artistic touch. Just as these sculptures, that represent firmness and hardness for their own sustenance through time.

The very sense of art, as we see it in these sculptures, is transferred to the observer in a tangible way. And not just by the fact that they can be touched, but by the idea that they can be felt. Art is felt, and not only by the tips of our fingers on that molded texture.

Watercolor Eyes

The only confusion of time is not wanting to assimilate the reality of a past: not wanting to value the foundational work of great artists who created coliseums, mausoleums, churches, walls, skyscrapers, entire societies.

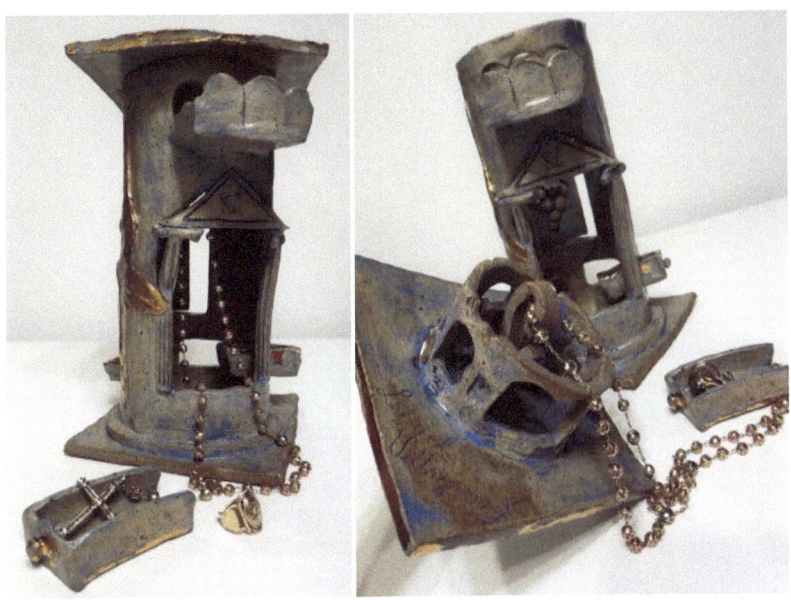

"There is no history without thinkers, and there are no thinkers without history." –Joshi

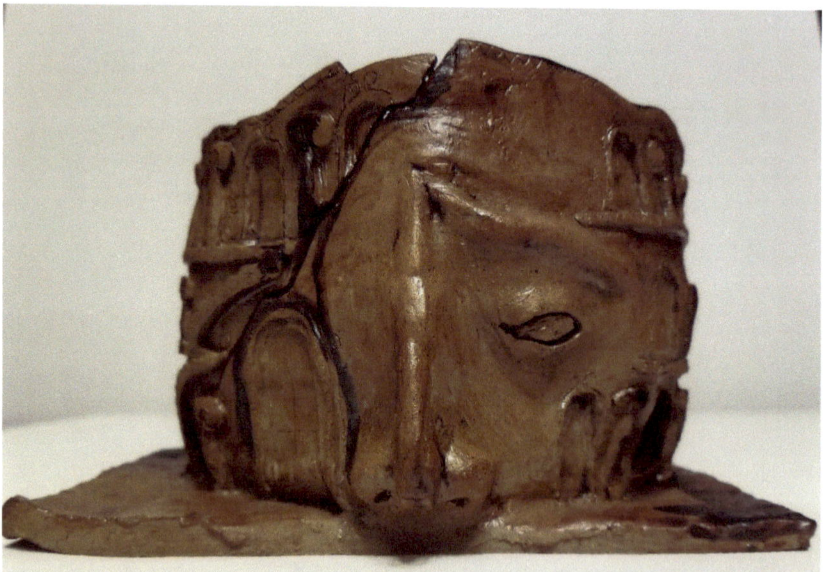

Leonel & Joshi Villagomez

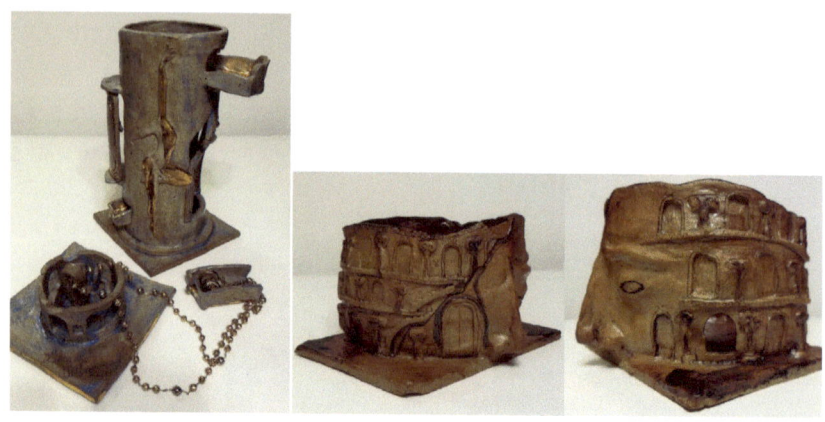

Watercolor Eyes

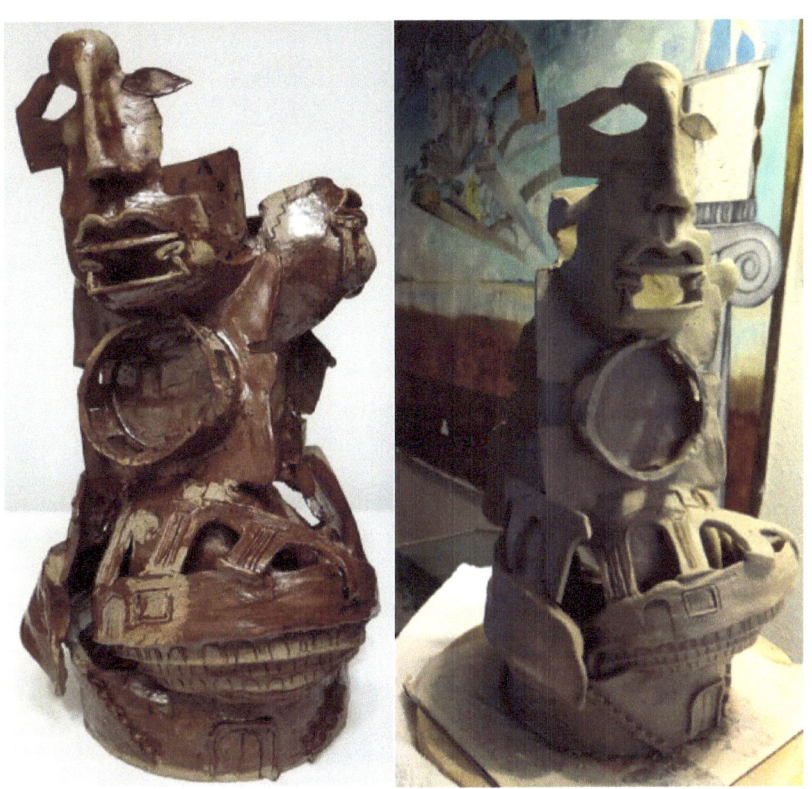

If he looks at these alone, the observer of art can question whether the molded works are precisely his preferred style, or if they deviate from a the central idea. Again, this is an interpersonal critique, where the appreciator of art can connect in a different and unique way to what another individual does. But that divine artistic appreciation develops through watercolor eyes.

XVIII.
The Extravagance of Saí

Salvador Dalí, a Spanish painter born in 1904, has heavily influenced the artist addressed in this book. However, the separation of style between Dalí and our artist appears in the imagination and context of their messages.

Surrealism is not a style exclusive to Salvador Dalí, but it is a cultural movement, emerged around 1920, that is most associated with Dalí. Published in October 1924, the *Manifeste du surréalisme* by Yvan Goll and André Breton opened the doors to a new era of art-making. With it, the exploration of the imagination and the appropriate ways to expose the unreal took traction in the practice of making art.

Let's take a step back and remember the work **"A colorful Dream"** from earlier in this book. What is its connection with reality, its contextual message? The dreams generated during the unconscious state of mind are an empirical example of how imagination plays a fundamental role in our lives. Not only does imagination exist within active creativity, but also within dreams.

If dreams are the reality of an artistic expression of life, then shouldn't surrealism be called not unreal, but normative?

Logical and generative applications fall on the beautiful artistic enigma to be fused to brushes and colors. Art is life and life is art.

Watercolor Eyes

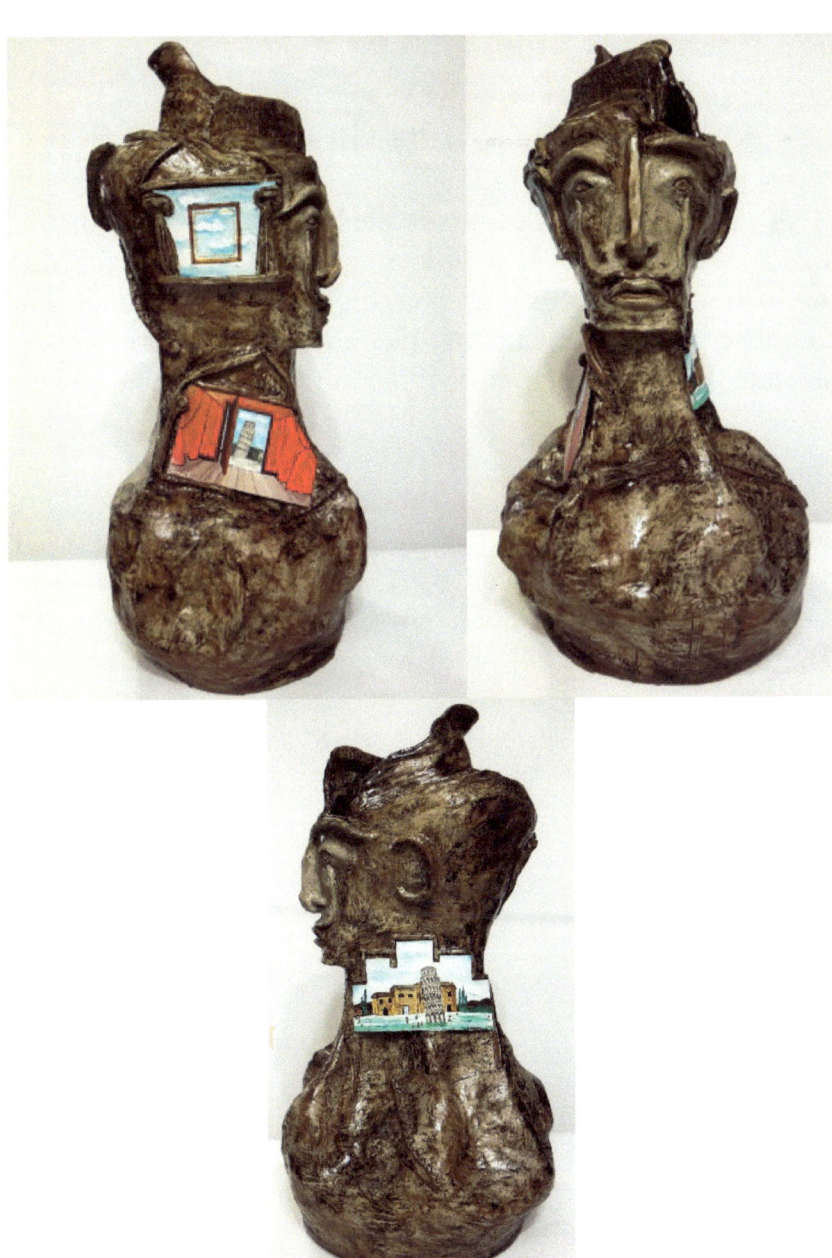

XIX.
The Artistic Mirage

A sensational idea, to see the balance of representation and realism. The following painting shows a mirror over a mirror. As you approach the painting, you can observe how the painting, like a shattered mirror, breaks and lets you see through it, as if the mirror were a type of wall.

The coordination of realism and surrealism expands with the context and the message that the author wishes to share: "I want the viewer to be the work of art when they look at themselves in the mirror," says Leonel Villagomez. An appropriate marriage of surrealism and ample imagination.

Again, through this surrealistic work of art, one must make a connection with the known, the observed, and what one intends to represent.

Watercolor Eyes

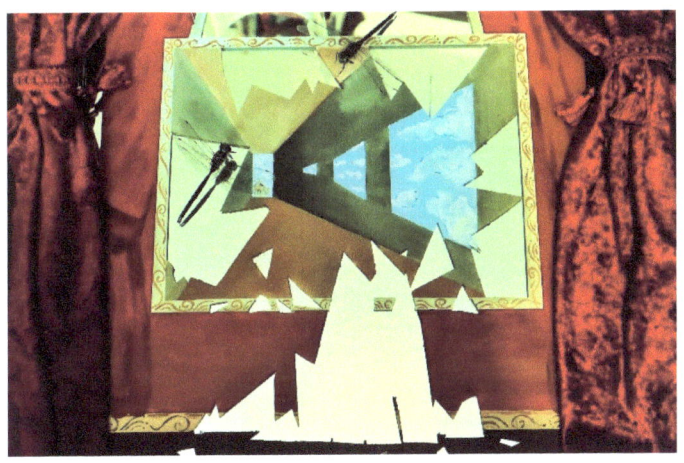

Leonel & Joshi Villagomez

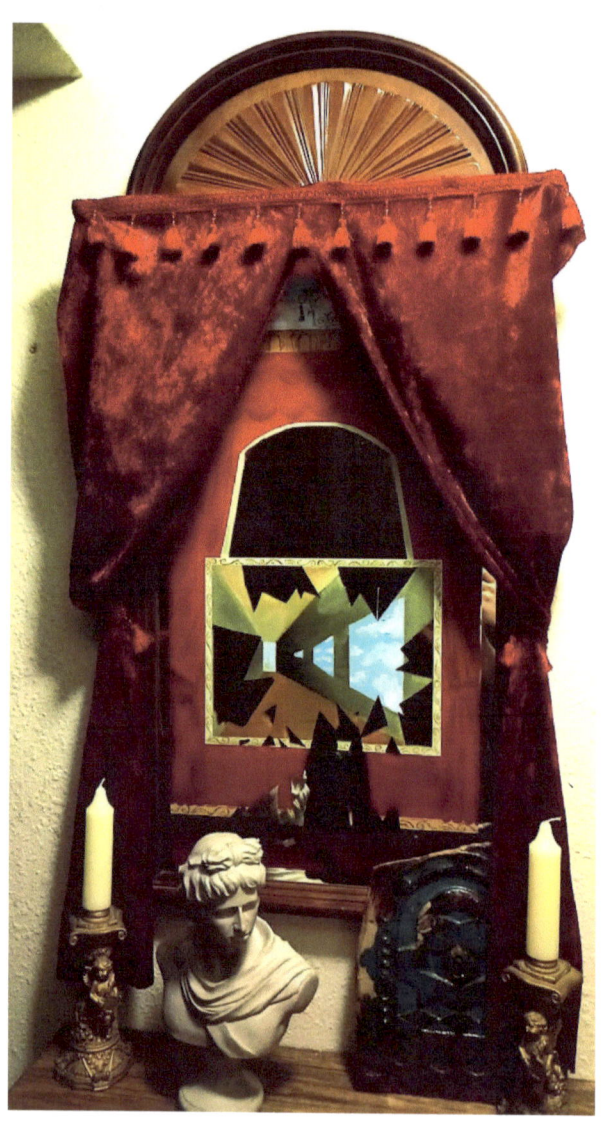

XX.
Letter to Juliet

Artistic and bohemian expressions expand the senses until they color the sensations, the emotions, the experiences, the knowledge of the known and unknown. As noted at the beginning of this book, we are part of the art around us. This art is not only symbolic, but it belongs to our past, our present, and our future.

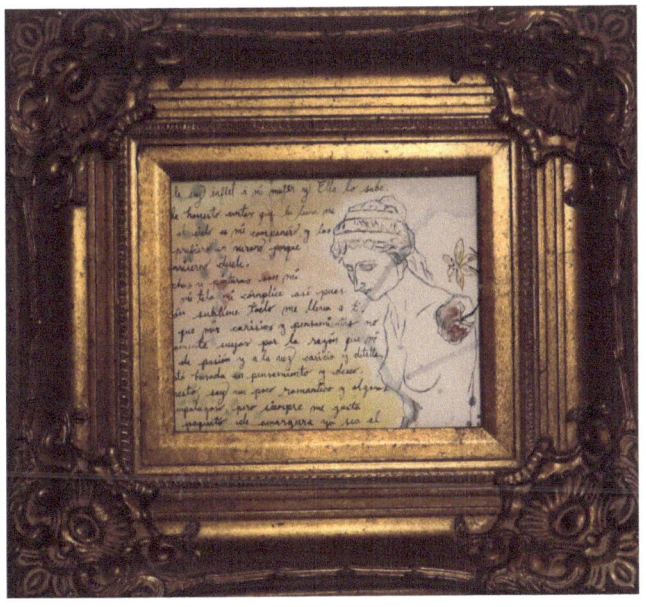

Our eyes, these watercolor eyes, dance with curiosity for discerning art, for colorful landscapes, and for diffused words that illuminate your mind when you read them. The journey is extended or limited by the way the observer appreciates things: with the way you change that melodic and sincere color through the pupil of your eyes. And without relying solely on emotional reactions, it depends on the observer how to value the art around him.

And whatever the message present in a work of art, it can exclaim as loudly and clearly as the words within a written treatise—but its message is embodied before those watercolor eyes.

The controversy, polemic, reason, or imagination described in verses, or in rational words, or in lies illustrated in surrealism, or in the enigmatic presence of molded clay or any other work of art, is life.

There would be no rules if there were no chaos. There would be no judges, if there were no people to judge. There would be no controversy, if we all thought the same things. And there would be no art if humanity did not exist.

The past, present, and future are shaped by the delicious dimensions that brighten our senses from dawn to dusk. There is no pain that lasts a hundred years, only the art that you don't appreciate in the same way as your neighbor. And if it is with a different relativity that you dare to accept the artistic work—as a biography of beauty--then there is no pain whatsoever.

And when you open your eyes every morning, just remember how to change that artistic perception. It is not enough just to live one more day, but to appreciate every detail throughout your day. And if, those watercolor eyes of yours, decide one

Watercolor Eyes

day to fall into silent blindness, just remember to draw yellow dragons in your imagination; and when you see yourself away from art and with nothing to observe you may say to yourself, "I have seen everything."

Leonel & Joshi Villagomez

XXI.
Other Works of Art

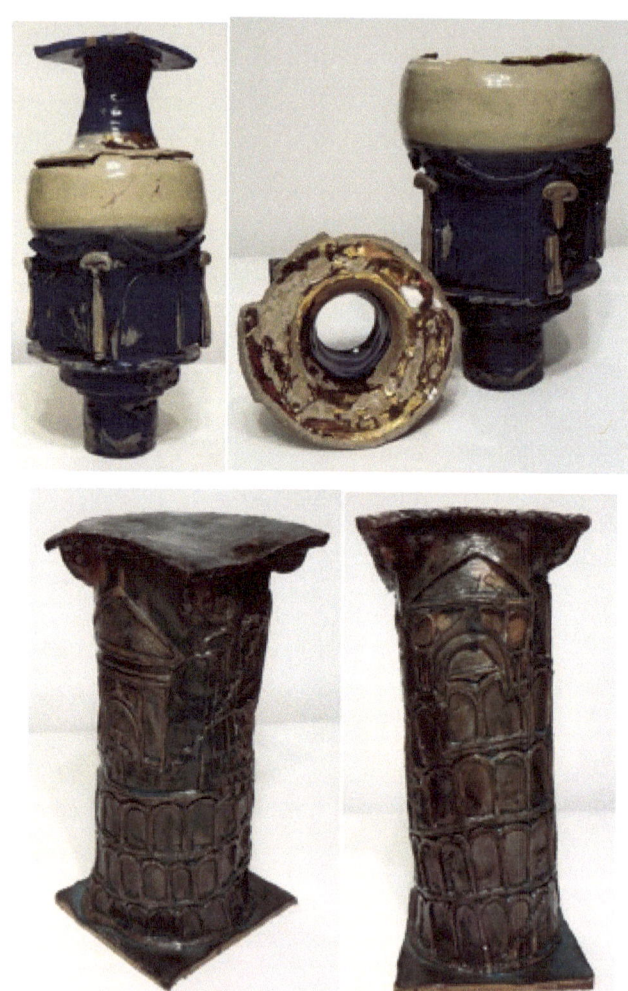

Watercolor Eyes

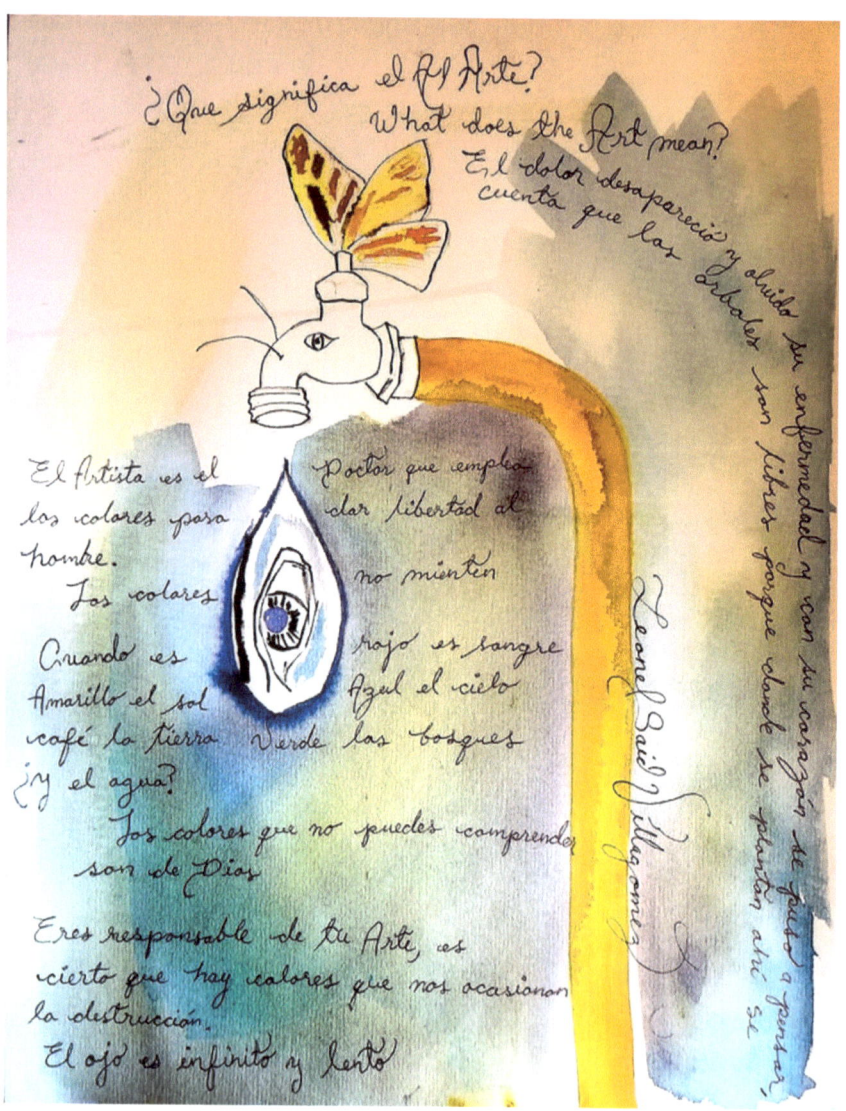

Watercolor Eyes

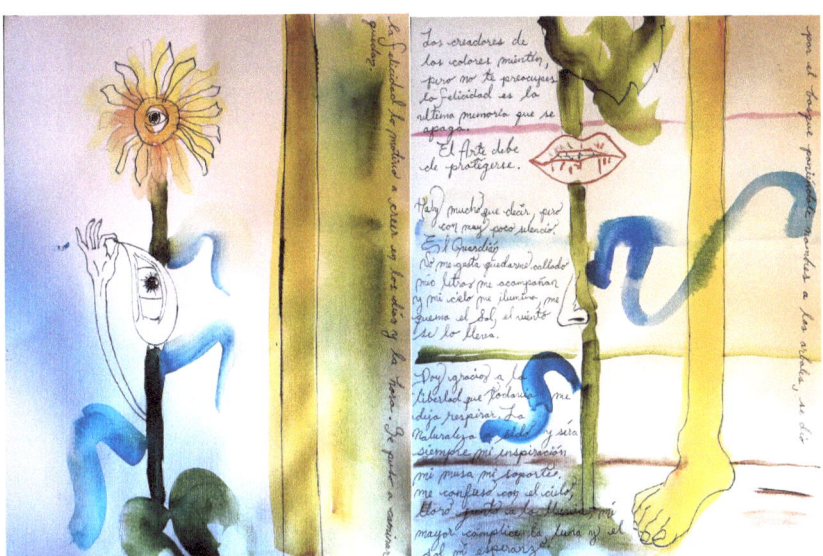

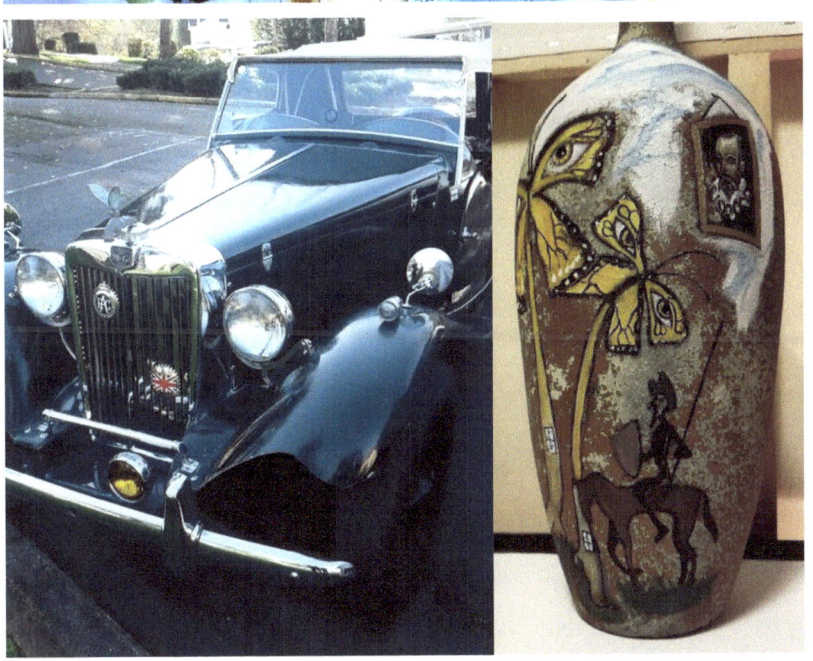

XXII.

Replicas

Whether by special orders or to participate in community events, these are some of the works recreated by Leonel.

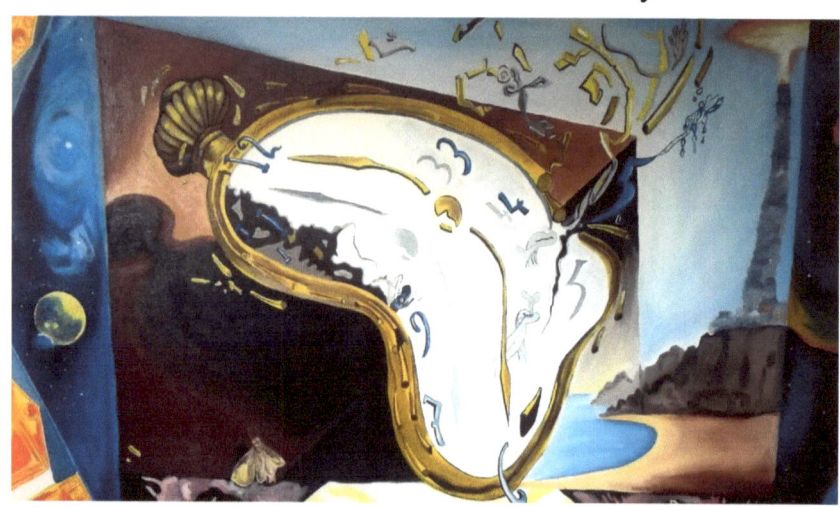

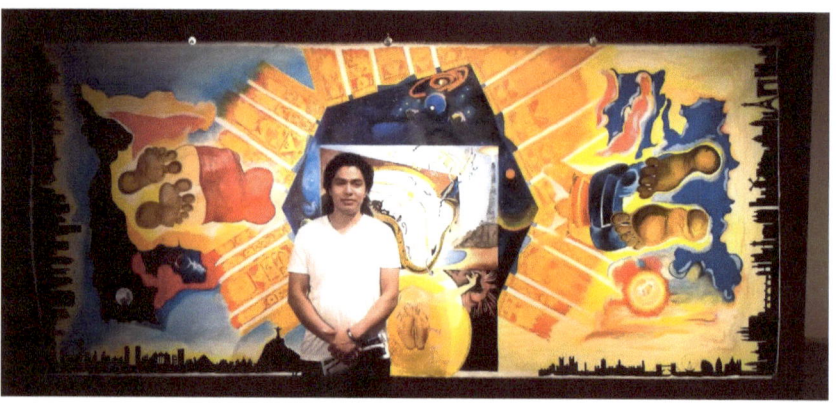

Watercolor Eyes

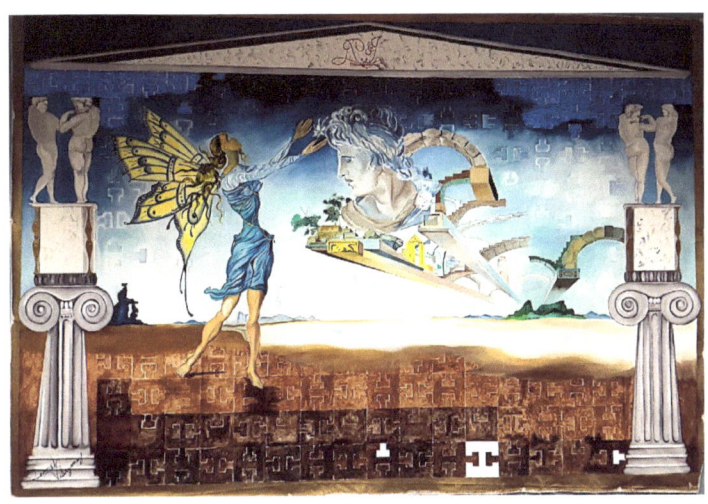

"This painting is inspired by Salvador Dali and, of course, by the angels of Michelangelo's Sistine Chapel, with a small detail of Roman architecture. I also added the 'Wings of Love.' As you can see, this painting is not complete due to the missing pieces of the puzzle at the bottom."
—Leonel

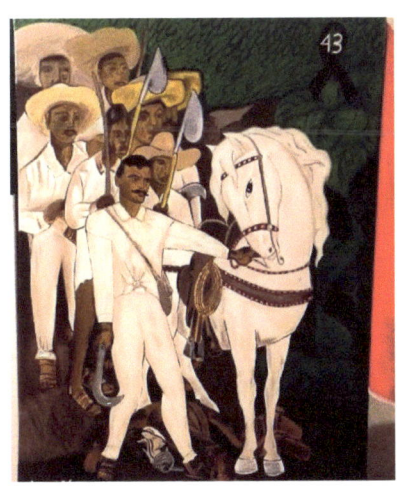
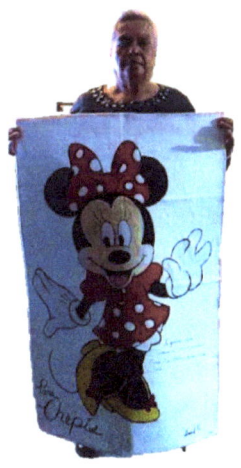

XXIII.
Biographies
Leonel Villagomez

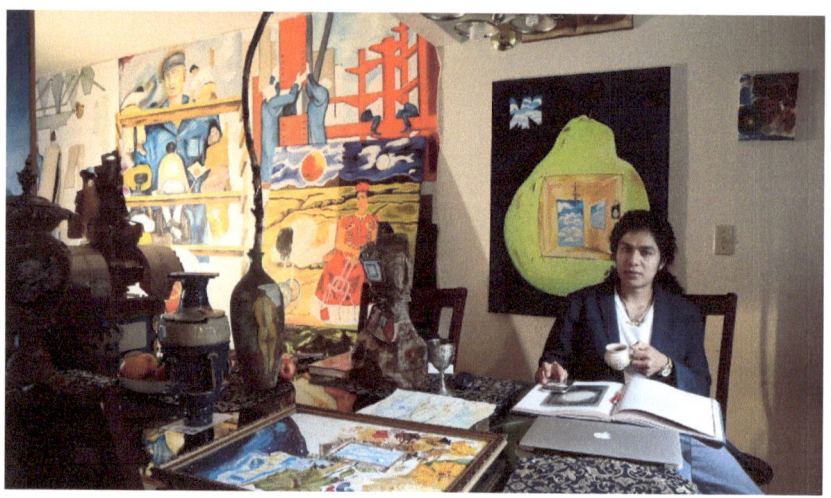

Leonel is an artist passionate about different techniques and artistic expressions such as Muralism, Surrealism, and Expressionism. From an early age he showed interest in Sacred Art, as well as in the great baroque and neoclassical architecture of the beautiful and eclectic city of Morelia, where he grew up. Visit his website to learn more about him.

www.villagomezart.com

Joshi Villagomez

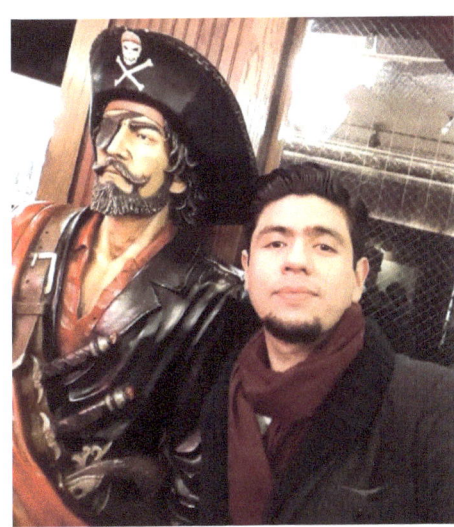

"I never know what I will be writing next, or to what length I should take my imagination in writing. I adore giving life to characters, thoughts and actions."

Joshi is contemporary writer that transforms ideas, issues, anecdotes, and life incidents into an allegorical life-narrative. Although he began writing only poetry, his interest in other forms and genres have continued to grow. Joshi has written dozens of poems in English and Spanish. He has written a few short stories, philosophical opinions about social issues and this book of art. To know more about him, visit his website.

www.joshivillagomez.com

Leonel & Joshi Villagomez

Watercolor Eyes by Leonel Villagomez & Joshi Villagomez
Independently Published. Seattle WA, USA.

www.joshivillagomez.com
&
www.villagomezart.com

Copyright © 2019 Leonel Villagomez & Joshi Villagomez

All rights reserved. No portion of this book may be reproduced in any form without permission from the publisher or the author, except as permitted by U.S. copyright law. Replicas are the intellectual property of their respective authors. For permissions contact:

writervillagomez@gmail.com

Art and Cover by Leonel Villagomez

ISBN: 9781796613308